BONE DUST

BONE DUST

RAYNE CORVUS MILLER

The Witches Altar

Trigger warnings for blood, violence, censorship, (thoughts of) death, sleep paralysis, religious trauma, gender dysphoria, and altered states of consciousness.

First Printing, 2023
Second Printing 2025

Edited by Elena Malkov
Designed by Rayne Corvus Miller

Published by The Witches Altar, LLC
www.thewitchesaltar.com

This book is dedicated to the Old Gods.

Contents

1

The Avalanche

Storm clouds pass over leafless treetops
        resonant, threatening,
like the avalanche of wisdom he ignores,
keeps behind closed doors.
The tree limbs reach skyward,
bent to the howling winds
and the thunder
that rattles his bones into dust.
Again and again, the infernal vibrations
erode, skin slipping,
dripping with the rains that started gently
but now carry him away.

2

Boneless

When the foundations crumbled
        into the churning black sea
and the temples burned to ash
the skies dared to be blue.

I killed the sun,
closed my eyes,
and fell.

I am boneless in the sea
floating, drowning, floating again,
each wave a pulse through my limp,
limp body.
My kingdom is aflame,
and I beg the dark waters to claim me.
But still I float.
Still I float.

Crows circle overhead.
Perhaps they think me dead,
for surely my soul perished in the fire.
They circle nearer,
so close I can see their manic eyes,
feel the beating of their wings,
flap, flap, flap...
Talons settle into my chest,
piercing my flesh, drawing blood,
and I am claimed.

When next I am conscious
I splutter the sands from my mouth,
tasting the ocean's salt.
I remember dreams of darkness,
a one-eyed man,
a half-dead girl...
I know these sands.
I peer through the limbs of the nearest tree
and see my realm reborn,
settled in the mountainside
beside a mighty waterfall catching a rainbow of light.

There is laughter and drumming,
horns and shouts of ecstasy
behind the wooden gates that yawn open.
I recognize nothing,
neither the spirits nor the sanctum,

none of the songs they sing.
I do not know the way,
but a warm hand takes mine
and the land proclaims my name.

3

Blood Brother

On the precipice between light and dark,
        there is a place
bathed in shadow and dusk,
and in dust, it rises.
In the in-between,
blurred lines beget blurred lines
beget freedom,
and he is complete where he is unchained
in the pit of torment and bliss.
Here, dimensions are many,
and they are his power,
firepower illuminating the path between paths
where the eclipsed soul finds itself again.

4

Fire & Brimstone

You may try
        to burn a witch at the stake
but they have learned
to walk through your flames:
they knows that hate
is born of love,
and that your fear
will undo you.

5

Nightclaimed

"From childhood's hour, I have not been
as others were."
I, lost in a skin-splitting pondering of humanhood.
I, a fright to the elder folk.
I, who the Night had claimed as Her own
long before my first taste of body and of blood.
Let the others feast upon unleavened lies;
my testament is older than the beginning.

6

In Darkness

I danced for you, once,
    with the ignorance of a child,
robed in white and salvation-high,
hiding the wilted and wild.

The dead turned my gaze,
and I shed my lies,
bare before the high king's throne,
I tried in vain to hide.

But visions passed and so did I
See clearly past black and white
To find a new name, a face of gray,
Allfather now in my sight.

Masked and robed and naked, too,
I dance for you once again,

This time I twirl in wisdom's glow.
In darkness, I will ascend.

7

War at Moonrise

I don't know if they're omens,
    the things that haunt my dreams.
There's blood and death and whispers
of truth, or so it seems.

I don't know if they're visions,
though sometimes they come true.
In sleep, I see the bodies,
the ghosts of me and you.

Once, I saw twin airplanes
rain havoc from the sky.
Another time, a sharp blade cut
the tracker from my eye.

My past once birthed a demon
that looked a lot like me.

I wore a crown of ice and thorn
and ruled on bended knee.

Hands pulled me by my ankles
'til soil filled my lungs.
I pulled the ladder with me,
broke every goddamn rung.

But worst is when I'm breathing
yet cannot seem to wake,
my body unresponsive
to every move I make.

In time, I see the sunrise
and start the war anew
Hammer raised to sacrifice
the ones without a clue.

8

Ode to Helheim

The dread sentence of death
    conveyed to my soul the idea of revolution.

I shuddered and fell
upon seven tall candles, white and slender.
I felt every fiber in my frame thrill
and thought of what sweet rest
there must be in the grave.

The darkness supervened,
a mad rushing descent into Hades.
Then silence, and stillness,
night were the universe.
All of consciousness was lost
in the deepest delirium.

We break.

We remember.
We return to life.

Shall we distinguish
the tomb come unbidden?
Sad visions ponder the meaning of never.

When I dreamed of success,
I conjured shadows and silence,
a vague horror as if all is madness,
the madness of forbidden things.

Blackout poem. Source text: "The Pit and the Pendulum" by Edgar Allan Poe.

9

Thorned One

The rose rises from thorns
     empty without those sharp
shameless daggers
held only by the careful
and the worthy
who respect the balance
between such pleasure,
such pain.

10

Lost Soul

My soul, perhaps, cannot *now* be my beloved.
     The thrills of the unknown
decay near ancient doubt,
deaden mine eyes,
my own passionate devotion.

I have utterly forgotten the spirit
emaciated in vain to portray
the incomprehensible slumbering souls
we have been falsely taught to worship.

Without some strangeness,
how cold, indeed, the regions above the temples.
The free spirit,
the triumph,
the magnificent ray of holy light,
scrutinized, possessed, forgotten.

We find ourselves upon the very verge of remembrance,
without being able, in the end, to remember.

Once, the universe passed into my spirit.
I felt aroused.
I felt the falling.
I felt the magnitude.
I have been filled with it by passages from books,
a great will pervading all things.

Man, that violent vulture of passion and of words
forced itself upon my attention.

The chaotic marriage of all that is ethereal
slows before me
gorgeous, untrodden,
a wisdom too precious to be forbidden.
How poignant the grief.
I — wanting the radiant luster of letters
golden upon the pages — grew ill,
became the waxen hue of the grave, grim and stern.
Resistance wrestled with the Shadow
amid the most convulsive writhings of spirit,
of mortal aspirations.

I doubted my passionate devotion, I,
cursed with the removal of my beloved.

Blackout poem. Source text: "Ligeia" by Edgar Allan Poe.

First published in 2023 under another name in

Dark Corners of the Old Dominion *by Death Knell Press.*

11

Sonnet of Death

Beneath the ground on which I tread
    Lie corpses of people past,
Those long gone, but not forgot,
With stories of their life's last.

The scent of death lingers in air,
Yet life, too, finds its home
Among the aging tombstones here
Where the immortal souls roam.

Stories filled with beauty and pain,
Friendship, temptation, and truth,
Surviving in memories still so alive
Beneath life's fragile roof.

What will we discover as we take our last breath?
There is, in fact, great beauty in death.

12

In the Gallows

He found me in the gallows — twice.
　　Once, when my knee
would no longer bend to the cross.
Again, when my soul burned from my body in protest.
He took me by the forearm and vowed
I would never know such agony again — *follow me.*
And the second time, I did.

Thirteen years he'd waited
knowing the gallows would greet me once more
after I wrapped myself in chains
and called it a dance.
I knew in my bones this life was not mine
yet I fought the reaper when he came for it.
Leave it — the hooded one urged.
And this time, I listened.

When the ax swung true, I did not flinch.
I hit the ground in pieces,
the chains clattering to the gallows' ground.
The old man and I did not look back
at the crutches I'd mistaken for a spine.
This time, I smiled.

13

❧

Seer's Prophecy

The midnight sun will burn above the graves.
The precious living will not dare to linger.
Only the ravens and spiders will see
Death's hand pierce the dirt.

14

Winter Winds

The mountainside drips mist
	through the snow-topped spruce
surrounding the great hall,
its doors carved with the world tree's roots.
Bare feet cross from bare dirt
to the rough wooden floor.

Silent footfalls reach the hof
where candle and incense burn,
a whispered oath, a raised horn,
and the distant storm thunders.
Winter winds ruffle
the banners that hang, and firelight
bows to Odin's breath.

He is here with you, voice-bearer,
worthy soul drenched in battle-sweat.

He is here, golden chalice held aloft,
a toast to ash and sacrifice.

The blood-swan croaks once.

15

The Way

Blue. Not tranquil, but burning,
    the hottest blaze of flame,
a body born without limits
yet strangled by perception.
This is the way.

Blood. Not pooled, but pounding,
beating to a disquiet rhythm,
demanding life, commanding it,
a simple truth made troublesome.
This is the way.

Stone. Not solid, but eroding,
sliced open by the steady stream
of all that cannot be contained,
of all that is without end.
This is the way.

Skin. Not smooth, but calloused
by the power of creation,
marking time with talismans
to remember the forgotten.
This is the way.

Bones. Not of the living,
but of Death himself and his skill
for reviving the decayed soul,
singeing it blue once more.
This is the way.

16

Old Bones

As the tallest tips of pine trees catch
    great Sunna's fading gleam,
the wise one sinks into the grass

The northern lights glow brighter
than the bonfire keeping
old bones warm in the growing night

Frogs and insects chatter
shadows fade into darkness
around the burning of logs and brush
crackling to accompany
the cacophony of dusk

The wise one exhales and ponders
what wonders the west might hold

Rayne Corvus Miller is an accomplished poet and writer who has performed their work on stages in both the United States and the United Kingdom. They are the author of *Bone Dust* and other wordsmithing found in *No Tomb of His Own, Dark Corners of the Old Dominion, The Spooklet, Lingering in the Margins, Parhelion Literary Magazine,* and more.

As co-host of *The Witches Table* podcast, Miller discusses Pagan and Heathen spirituality along with how it intersects with their writing life. They are a member of the *Horror Writers Association* and *Trans Journalists Association.*

You can follow their work at meadofpoetry.art.

www.ingramcontent.com/pod-product-compliance
Lightning Source LLC
Chambersburg PA
CBHW010335150726
47988CB00022BA/3537